D0929839

This journal belongs to:

About the Artist

Jess Volinski is a graduate of the School of Visual Arts in New York, NY, and the author/illustrator of more than a dozen coloring & activity books, including *Notebook Doodles® Super Cute, Notebook Doodles® Go Girl!*, and *Notebook Doodles® Sweets & Treats*. Besides creating books, she currently licenses her art for the publishing, fashion, and tableware industries. Originally from Connecticut, Jess now lives in southern New Jersey with her husband and two kids.

Other Notebook Doodles® Activity Books

ISBN 978-1-64178-038-4

Fox Chapel Publishing makes every effort to use environmentally friendly paper for printing.

© 2018 by Jess Volinski and Quiet Fox Designs, *www.QuietFoxDesigns.com*, an imprint of Fox Chapel Publishing, 800-457-9112, 903 Square Street, Mount Joy, PA 17552.

We are always looking for talented authors. To submit an idea, please send a brief inquiry to acquisitions@foxchapelpublishing.com.

Printed in China
First printing